101 SCIENCE POEMS & SONGS for Young Learners
With Hands-on Activities

by Meish Goldish

SCHOLASTIC
PROFESSIONAL BOOKS

New York • Toronto • London • Auckland • Sydney

Design by Liza Charlesworth and Jaime Lucero for Grafica, Inc.

Cover design by Jaime Lucero and Vincent Ceci

Illustrations by Bari Weissman

ISBN 0-590-96369-4

Contents

Continued on the next page

Welcome to *101 Science Poems and Songs for Young Learners*. Children have a natural curiosity about bears, clouds, flowers, stars, magnets, and fossils—in other words, science. These easy poems and songs provide a fun way to reinforce many basic science concepts by tapping into children's love for verse, rhythm, and music. These forget-proof rhymes build literacy as they add a sprinkle of fun and facts to your curriculum. Enjoy!

How to Use This Book

The poems in this book are divided into six categories so you can easily find a poem to fill a particular need. The poems and songs are divided into these categories:

◆ **The Earth and Beyond:** Earth and space-science related poems.

◆ **Plants and Seeds:** Rhymes about green plants, flowers, and seeds.

◆ **Animals, Animals:** Critters galore, along with poems about animal homes and behaviors.

◆ **The Human Body:** Poems about organs, the senses, digestion, and germs.

◆ **Seasons and Weather:** The water cycle, ice, summer, and clouds are featured in these poems.

◆ **More Science Wonders:** Physical-science related poems about sound, magnets, gravity, and density.

The poems can be used as part of a particular science unit, for example, having students read *Solar System in Motion* as part of your unit on space. Also, these science poems can be incorporated into everyday activities like any other verse. For instance, use them as a way to start or end the day, or re-focus after recess; as part of a classroom poetry corner; or as a way to transition into science time.

There are many ways to make poems easier to remember and more fun to read. Allowing students to repeat lines back to you in a call and response fashion; letting children tap out the poem or song's rhythm with feet, hands, or rhythm instruments; having student groups read poems together by alternating lines; and inviting students to record poems on tape—all add to a poem's impact. Of course, there's really no right or wrong way to use the poems in this book. You, as the teacher, know how your students best respond and learn. However, below you'll find some suggested activities for extending learning using the poems as launch pads for projects, celebrations, literature related activities, and simple science experiments.

Activities to Extend Learning

Take it Further: When reading a particular poem in class, think about taking it a bit further and/or reinforcing the science content by asking questions or challenging students to add verses. This is a great way to check comprehension and give students the opportunity to include their own knowledge about a topic. Many of the poems and songs naturally bring up questions. For example: What kinds of animals might live in the caves, farms, and holes mentioned in *Animal Homes*? Many of the poems also lend themselves to calling for more examples, such as: What else makes *Light*? What other sounds do animals make besides those in *Animal Talk*? Can you name other kinds of *Rock*?

Celebrate Seasons and Earth Day: The poems *Winter*, *Spring*, *Summer*, *Fall* are perfect for celebrations of the changing calendar. Student groups can present them to the class, they can be displayed with accompanying decorations on bulletin boards, or given as take-home reading. Likewise, *Save Our Animals* and *Recycling* are excellent for Earth Day activities.

Poster Poetry: Nearly all of the poems and songs can be made into terrific posters by student groups or individuals. Here are some ideas:

◆ Ask students to write the poem's text in large letters on poster board and then decorate its border with things mentioned in the poem. This is a creative way to bring the verses alive, and works especially well with many of the "listing" poems like *Rock*, *Desert*, *Fruits*, *Planet Roll Call*, or *Vegetables*.

◆ Lines from poems that infer step-by-step processes like *Mountain*, *Birth of a Butterfly*, *Water Cycle*, and *Digestion* can be used as captions to illustrations of successive steps. For example, invite students to draw the stages of a butterfly's life on posterboard and then choose lines from *Birth of a Butterfly* as captions.

◆ Have students choose lines from descriptive poems like *Pollination*, *Parts of a Flower*, *Five Senses*, and *Animal Defenses* to use as labels on diagrams they've drawn on posterboard.

◆ Encourage students to use animal group poems such as *Mammals*, *Reptiles*, *Amphibians*, *Bugs*, *Birds*, and *Fish* as part of descriptive posters that list the animal group's characteristics and illustrate some representative members.

Mobile Poetry: Many of the poems can be made into moving art, or mobiles. Have student groups cut out or draw representative shapes, label them with lines from a poem, and then assemble them into mobiles. For example, *Planet Roll Call* makes great labels for a mobile of planets as does *Flight* for types of flight. *Fruits* and *Vegetables* provide lots of examples of shapes that students can cut out and assemble into mobiles.

Poetry Theater and Puppet Plays: A number of the poems and songs lend themselves to being acted out such as *My Body* ("Jump, twirl, bend, whirl...") and *Solar System in Motion* ("The moon goes round the Earth"). Other poems like *Desert*, *Rainforest*, *Astronaut*, and *Planet Roll Call* can be converted into finger puppet plays. Students can create finger puppet characters of the animals, planets, and so forth who speak lines or describe themselves.

Mini-Books: Invite students to make a mini-book out of a science poem. Each line or stanza can be written on a separate page and then illustrated. Creating a cover with an appropriate shape is a natural for poems about animals or others like *Flowers*, *Moon*, *Cloud*, and *Bones*. Shorter poems can also be copied in their entirety on paper shaped to reflect their theme.

Be a Poet: Reading and "playing" with the poems in this book will inspire the poet in all your students, so encourage them by setting aside time for poem writing. Besides asking students or student groups to add additional lines or stanzas to their favorite poems, challenge them to write poems of their own on a given topic. Acrostic poems are great for younger kids and reluctant poets and many of the poem's titles like *Stars, Ocean, Echo, Birds, Winter*, etc., make good ones. Students can present their poems to the class, display them on a wall, or create mini-books or shape pages out of them.

Literature Links: The short science poems in this book introduce basic science concepts. As your students begin to crave more information and depth on a particular topic, turn to some of the Book Links on page 95 to satisfy them. The books listed are arranged in the same categories as the poems and songs, and are directly linked to them. For example, Rauzon's *Horns, Antlers, Fangs, and Tusks* compliments the poem *Animal Defenses*; Branley's *The Moon Seems to Change* builds on the poem *Moon*; and Browne's *No Problem* is about machines, and adds to *Machine Song*. The books can be read aloud in class or simply made available to interested students.

Poetic Experiments: Science principles are best learned and remembered when experienced first hand. Many of the poems and songs in this book are great launching points for simple hands-on experiments. To follow are a few, with the title of a related poem provided in parentheses.

The Earth and Beyond

Sun Strength: (*Sun*) Students can observe the sun's power by watching how colored construction paper fades. Have students place a piece of colored construction paper on a sunny windowsill. Ask them to arrange objects like coins, erasers, cups, etc., on the

paper. (Make sure they use objects that won't be easily knocked off or blown away.) Leave the papers on the windowsill for a week or two then invite students to predict what the paper will look like underneath the objects. Let them remove their objects to confirm or disprove their predictions. The areas protected from sunlight have kept their color. However, the strong sunlight has broken down the paper's dyes in the exposed areas and faded it.

Weigh Air: (*Air*) Students observe that even though air is invisible, we know it exists because it has weight. Make a "set of scales" by hanging a 10-inch piece of heavy string off the edge of a table or door frame. Tape it there. Tie a loop in the dangling end big enough for a flat ruler to go through. Slide a ruler through and then place a teaspoon or so of modeling clay on one end of the ruler and attach an inflated balloon to the other. Adjust the ruler by sliding it back and forth till it balances without being held. Ask your students: What's in the balloon? (Air.) Does it weigh anything? (Yes.) Next carefully deflate the balloon by piercing it near the knot. The clay side drops without the weight of the balloon's air to balance it.

Plants and Seeds

Key Trees: (*Growth of a Tree*) Students determine that trees can be identified by their leaves. Challenge students to bring in six different kinds of tree leaves from their yard or a neighborhood park. Then provide students with simple tree keys to assist them in determining what kinds of trees they have found. Invite students to make a book of their leaves, illustrating them with drawings of the trees. The leaves can be preserved on the pages by covering them with clear contact paper.

Plant Needs: (*Plants*) Students discover the needs of green plants by experimenting with growing conditions. Divide students into groups and assign each a growing condition: light, air, space, water, or nutrients. Each group's task is to grow two identical plants in an identical way except for a variation in their particular condition. For example, the Air Group would plant bean seeds in identical cups with identical soil, set them in identical sunlight and water equally, but one would be placed in a plastic bag with all the air removed by a straw and sealed, while the other would not. After a few weeks, have each group report on how their plants fared and hypothesize why.

Animals, Animals

Underground Neighbors: (*Underground Creatures*) Students observe what lives underground in common soil. Collect about a quart of soil from outside. Line the bottom of a large glass mixing bowl with wet paper towels and set a pasta strainer inside the bowl. Then put the soil into the strainer. Set a bright lamp over the dirt-filled strainer and leave the lamp on all night. The next day pick up the strainer. Invite students to observe with hand lenses all the creepy crawlies that have wriggled out during the night. Students can draw the bugs and try to identify them.

Hatch Away: (*Eggs*) Students observe what hatches out of different eggs. Collect or purchase eggs that can be hatched out in class with minimal fuss. Frog eggs and some fish eggs work well as do various kinds of insect eggs, and of course chicken eggs in an incubator. (Bait shops often carry viable eggs as do biological supply companies.) Assign groups of students to each kind of egg and have them report to the class every few days on any changes they observe. Invite the students in each group to keep a diary of the creature's progress out of its egg.

The Human Body

Sense It: (*Five Senses*) Students use their five senses to describe a piece of fruit. List the five senses—sight, smell, touch, hearing, and taste—on the board. Then hand out a piece of fruit to each student. Challenge students to use each of their senses in turn to describe their fruit: What does it look like? What does it smell like? What does it feel like—inside and out? What sound does it make when you gently tap it against your desk and when you bite into it? What does it taste like? Students can write down their observations for comparison after snacking on their fruit.

Rubber Bones: (*Bones*) Students discover one of the components needed for strong bones—calcium. Place a cleaned chicken bone in a jar full of white vinegar (the vinegar needs to completely cover the bone). Put a second similar chicken bone in an empty jar. Cap the lids tightly. After at least a week (two weeks if they're thick leg bones) take out the bones. Invite students to compare the two and ask:

What do you think makes bones strong? (Minerals, especially calcium.) What happened to the bone in the vinegar? (The calcium was leeched out by the vinegar and left the bone weak.)

Seasons and Weather

Create Clouds: (*Cloud*) Students observe how a cloud forms. Pour about 1/2 inch of very hot water into a clean, clear bottle with a narrow neck. Immediately cover the mouth of the bottle with an ice cube. Ask: What happens? (Inside the bottle a cloud of water vapor forms.) Why? (The hot water evaporates, rises and runs into the air cold from the ice and thus condenses into a cloud.)

Weather Maps: (*Weather*) Students determine the weather in different parts of the country by reading a weather map. Provide groups of students with a weather map from the newspaper. Point out the symbols identified in the legend and make sure all understand them. Then ask each group to report that day's weather for four different cities—New York, Los Angeles, Chicago and Houston, for instance—plus their own.

More Science Wonders

Attract a Magnet: (*Magnet*) Students experiment to discover what materials are magnetic. Have groups of students gather up some things they think might stick to magnets—coins, nails, paper clips, erasers, marbles, etc. Hand out a magnet to each group and challenge them to test each item, keeping track of those that are attracted to the magnet and those that aren't. Invite the groups to share their findings with the class.

Boats Float: (*Floating and Sinking*) Students discover how density affects floating and sinking. Ask student pairs to make two same-sized balls out of modeling clay. Then have them drop one into a large bowl or pan of water. Ask: Does it float? (No.) Why? (Clay is denser than water. A cup of clay weighs more than a cup of water.) Next challenge students to make a "boat" out of the other ball of clay so that it will float on the water. Once they have succeed, ask: What makes the same ball of clay float now? (The boat is filled with air. Together the air and clay mix is less dense than the clay only, and it is less dense than water—so it floats!)

Our World

The grass is green,
The sky is blue,
The moon is white,
The clouds are, too.
The sun is yellow,
The trees are brown,
The leaves are red
When falling down.
The sunset's orange,
The air is clear,
What a colorful world
We have right here!

In the Earth

On the earth,
What do you see?
Grass and trees
And the deep blue sea.
In the earth,
What do you see?
Metal and rock
As hot as can be!

Ocean

(sung to "Take Me Out to the Ball Game")

Take me out to the ocean,
Take me out to the sea.
Show me the foamy waves rolling there,
As I breathe in the salty sea air!

Let me look, look, look at the ocean,
See the sea and explore,
For it's fun to dive from the top
To the ocean floor!

Take me out to the ocean,
Take me out to the sea.
Show me the currents and ocean tides,
Let me see where the seaweed resides!

When you look, look, look at the ocean,
Look at all it is worth!
For the ocean covers three-fourths
Of the entire earth!

Sand

Sand at the beach,
Sand at the shore.
Sand in the ocean
On the ocean floor.

Sand in the desert,
Sand on the ground.
Sand in a sandstorm
Blowing around!

Sand from rock that has
Crumbled into grains
Sand in a sand dune
Shaped by wind and rains.

Sand on an island,
Sand in the sea.
Sand in a sandbox
For you and me!

Cave

I've come to a big room
Underground.
What have I found?
What have I found?
Walls of rock
Are all around.
What have I found?
What have I found?
It's damp and dark.
I must be brave!
Bats are around!
Bats are around!
What have I found?
I've found a cave!
That's what I've found!
That's what I've found!

River

By a river I see:
Fishes swimming,
Tankers floating,
Fishers fishing,
Boaters boating,
Bridges rising,
Waters flowing.
Life on the river
Keeps on going!

Rock

Rock rock.
Who's there?
Slate.
Slate who?
It's slate. Time to go to bedrock!

Rock rock.
Who's there?
Granite.
Granite who?
Don't take all rocks for granite!

Rock rock.
Who's there?
Coal.
Coal who?
If you're coal, I'll warm you up!

Rock rock.
Who's there?
Marble.
Marble who?
That pretty rock looks marble-ous!

Fossils

I dug in the ground
And my hand took hold
Of a dinosaur bone
That was very, very old!

I dug in the ground
And my hand took hold
Of a rocky leaf print
That was very, very old!

I dug in the ground
And my hand took hold
Of a stone-hard shell
That was very, very old!

I dug in the ground
And guess what I found?
Good old fossils!

Mountain

(sung to "She'll Be Comin' Round the Mountain")

Do you know what forms a mountain when it forms?
Do you know what forms a mountain when it forms?
First the earth starts moving slowly,
So that ground once flat and lowly
Pushes up and forms a mountain when it forms.

Do you know what's on a mountain that we use?
Do you know what's on a mountain that we use?
We use water, grass, and wood there,
And the climbing's also good there,
There's a lot upon a mountain that we use!

Do you know the tallest mountain in the world?
Do you know the tallest mountain in the world?
It's Mount Everest, in Asia,
Five miles high! (Does that amaze ya'?!)
Everest is the tallest mountain in the world.

Air

What can't you see
And yet it's there?
Air!
What do you breathe
Everywhere?
Air!
Can you live without air?
No, you can't!
Every person,
Animal, and plant
Needs the thing
That's beyond compare:
Air!

Desert

Out in the desert
So hot and dry,
You may see a camel
Or lizard pass by.
You may see a snake
Or a fox or an owl.
A hungry coyote
May be on the prowl.
Out in the desert,
So hot and dry,
Look and see
Who is passing by!

Rainforest

(sung to "I've Been Working on the Railroad")

I've been walking in the rainforest,
All among the trees.
I've been walking in the rainforest,
Where I saw the bats and bees.
Parrots, butterflies, and toucans,
Monkeys and hummingbirds galore.
Frogs and snakes and spotted leopards
On the rainforest floor!

I've been walking in the rainforest,
All among the green.
I've been walking in the rainforest,
Where the plant life must be seen!
Ferns and mosses and lianas,
Orchids and honeysuckle, too.
Oh, how special is the rainforest,
A magic place come true!

A new poem by

Shel Silverstein

for The Trumpet Club

LESSON

I didn't invite my barber to my party,
And I learned a lesson I would like to share—
If you don't invite your barber to your party,
Do *not* go back to him to cut your hair.

S.S.

SPECIAL TEAR-OUT SECTION

Day Sky

Look up high.
See the sky.
Fluffy clouds
Are floating by.
Graceful birds
Swiftly fly.
Sunshine beams
To keep earth dry.
Sky of blue
Makes me sigh!

Night Sky

Look up high.
See the sky.
Twinkling stars
Catch my eye.
Watchful owls
Hoot nearby.
Moonlight glows
On a firefly.
The sky is dark.
Me, oh, my!

Day and Night

The sun is always shining bright,
Always shining bright.
It shines on Earth to give us light,
The sun gives us light.
When the sunshine comes our way,
That's the time that we call day.
We go to school and work and play
In the light of day.

The sun is always shining bright,
Always shining bright.
So why do we have dark and night?
Why the dark and night?
When the Earth turns from the sun,
We get no light, and day is done.
We get no light, and night's begun.
Goodnight, everyone!

Sun

If I were the sun,
I'd have such fun!
I'd shine so bright
On everyone.
I'd be a ball
Of glowing gas.
I'd be a star
With giant mass!
I'd warm the plants,
I'd warm the Earth.
I'd show how much
My rays are worth!

Sunrise and Sunset

Why does the sun rise at sunrise?
Why does it come up so bright?
The sun doesn't rise at sunrise.
It's Earth that turns toward its light.

Why does the sun set at sunset?
Why does it drop out of sight?
The sun doesn't set at sunset.
It's Earth that turns from its light.

Stars

(sung to "Twinkle, Twinkle, Little Star")

Twinkle, twinkle, little star,
I know what you really are:
Giant ball of glowing gas,
One of billions in a mass!
Twinkle, twinkle, little star,
Oh, how big you really are!

Twinkle, twinkle, giant star,
Larger than the Earth by far!
Since your distance is a lot,
You look like a tiny dot.
Twinkle, twinkle, giant star,
Very bright, yet very far!

Stars are twinkling, every one,
Some are bigger than the sun!
Just a twinkle in the sky,
Just because you're oh, so high!
Twinkle, twinkle, little star,
Oh, how big you really are!

Shooting Star

Zoom!
It's a shooting star!
Zoom!
Quick as a wink!
Zoom!
Traveling fast and far!
Zoom!
Don't blink!

Moon

Are you lonely, Moon?
You giant white balloon!
You have no water, wind, or air.
No wonder nothing lives up there!
You can't grow trees or flowers or grass.
Your soil is only rocks and glass.
Even your light is not your own.
Instead it's from the sun that's shone.
Your gravity is weak, I hear.
You really have no atmosphere.
But don't be sad, Moon, please don't cry,
For I still love you in the sky.

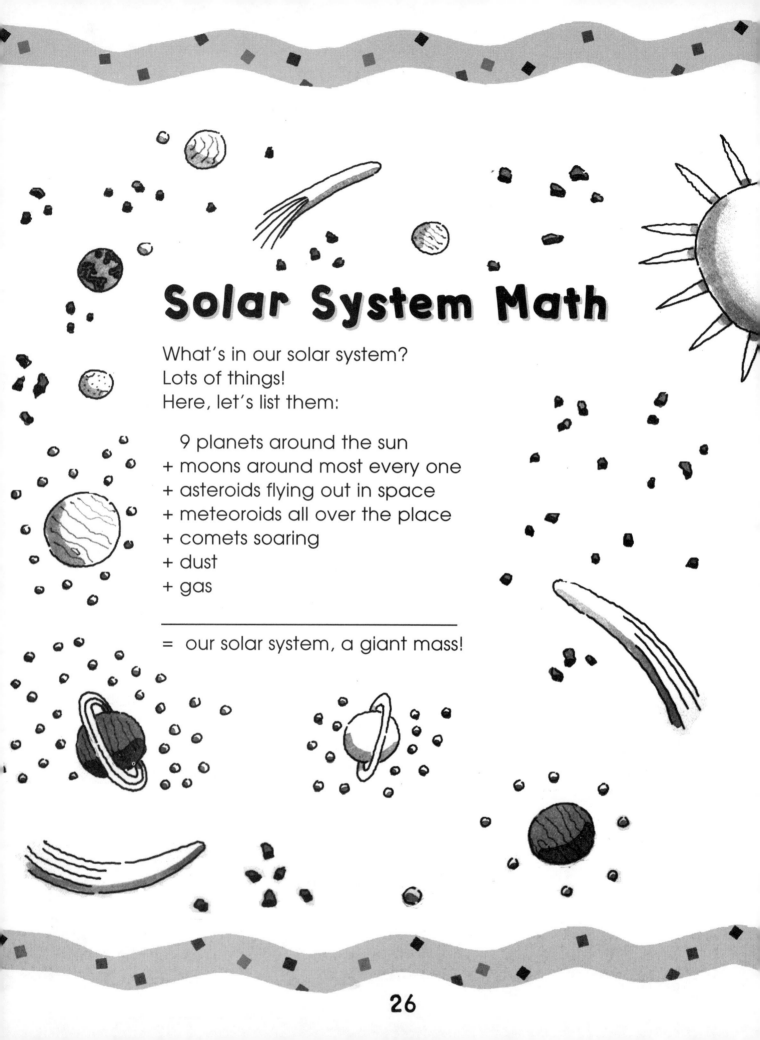

Solar System Math

What's in our solar system?
Lots of things!
Here, let's list them:

  9 planets around the sun
+ moons around most every one
+ asteroids flying out in space
+ meteoroids all over the place
+ comets soaring
+ dust
+ gas
_____
= our solar system, a giant mass!

Solar System in Motion

(sung to "The Farmer in the Dell")

The Earth turns around,
The Earth turns around.
Once a day, every day,
The Earth turns around.

The moon goes round the Earth,
The moon goes round the Earth.
Once a month, every month,
The moon goes round the Earth.

The Earth goes round the sun,
The Earth goes round the sun.
Once a year, every year,
The Earth goes round the sun.

27

Planet Roll Call

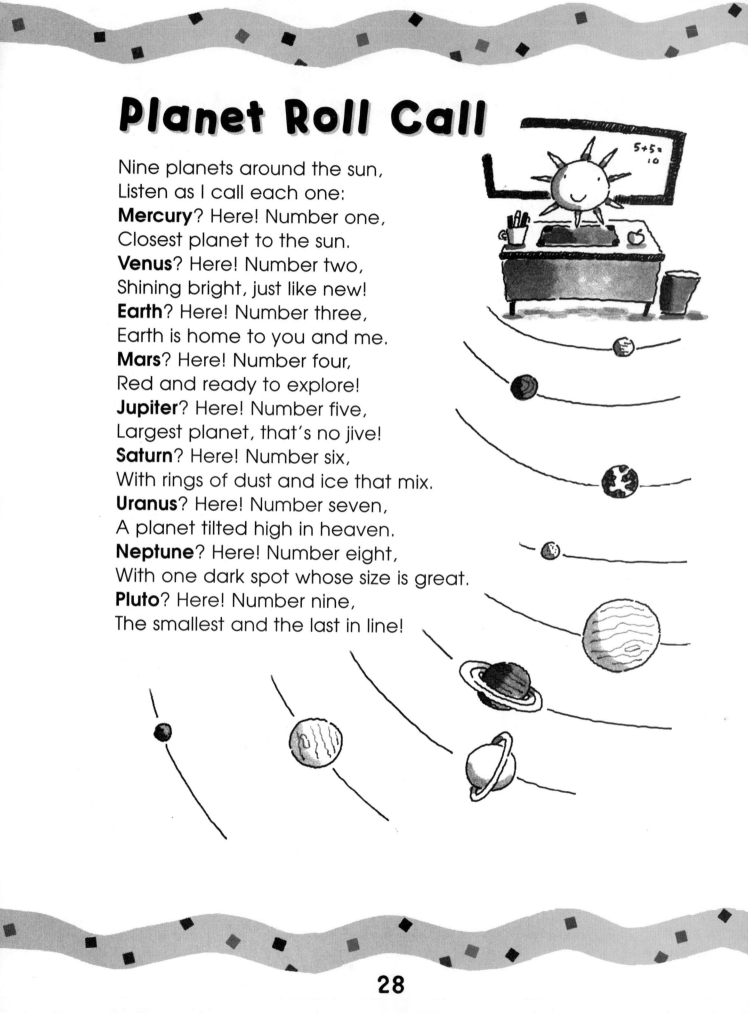

Nine planets around the sun,
Listen as I call each one:
Mercury? Here! Number one,
Closest planet to the sun.
Venus? Here! Number two,
Shining bright, just like new!
Earth? Here! Number three,
Earth is home to you and me.
Mars? Here! Number four,
Red and ready to explore!
Jupiter? Here! Number five,
Largest planet, that's no jive!
Saturn? Here! Number six,
With rings of dust and ice that mix.
Uranus? Here! Number seven,
A planet tilted high in heaven.
Neptune? Here! Number eight,
With one dark spot whose size is great.
Pluto? Here! Number nine,
The smallest and the last in line!

Astronaut

(sung to "Where Have You Been, Billy Boy?")

Tell me, where have you been,
Astronaut, astronaut?
Tell me, where have you been
In your rocket?
I have landed on the moon,
And I may return there soon
With a space station
That will help me dock it!

Tell me, what did you do,
Astronaut, astronaut?
Tell me, what did you do
In your rocket?
I took pictures of the stars
And the craters found on Mars,
And I brought home some moon rocks
In my pocket!

Green Plants

(sung to "Row, Row, Row Your Boat")

Grow, grow, grow your plants,
Grow with lots of care.
Carefully, carefully place your plants
Where they will get air.

Grow, grow, grow your plants,
Growing can be fun!
Carefully, carefully place your plants
Where they will get sun.

Grow, grow, grow your plants,
Never let them spoil.
Carefully, carefully place your plants
In a healthy soil.

Grow, grow, grow your plants,
One more thing to do:
Carefully, carefully give your plants
Lots of water, too!

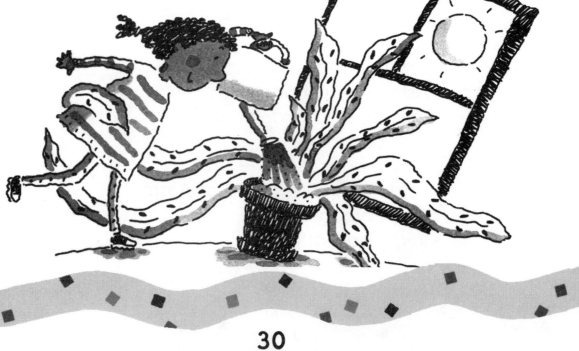

Parts of a Plant

(sung to "The Wheels on the Bus")

The roots on a plant grow underground,
Underground, underground.
The roots on a plant grow underground,
Roots are part of a plant.

The stems on a plant hold up the leaves,
Up the leaves, up the leaves.
The stems on a plant hold up the leaves,
Stems are part of a plant.

The leaves on a plant are making food,
Making food, making food.
The leaves on a plant are making food,
Leaves are part of a plant.

The flowers on a plant are growing seeds,
Growing seeds, growing seeds.
The flowers on a plant are growing seeds,
Flowers are part of a plant.

Flowers

Roses are red,
Violets are blue,
Flowers are rainbows of colors,
It's true!
Bright yellow sunflowers,
Orange touch-me-nots,
Pretty pink peonies
Planted in pots.
Lavender lilacs,
Zinnias bright green,
White garden lilies
Like you've never seen!
Goldenrods gold,
Bluebells so blue,
Rainbows of flowers
For me and for you!

Growth of a Tree

(sung to "I'm a Little Teapot")

I'm a little maple, oh so small,
In years ahead, I'll grow so tall!
With a lot of water, sun, and air,
I will soon be way up there!

Deep inside the soil my roots are found,
Drinking the water underground.
Water from the roots my trunk receives,
Then my trunk starts making leaves.

As I start to climb in altitude,
Leaves on my branches will make food.
Soon my trunk and branches will grow wide,
And I'll grow more bark outside!

I will be a maple very tall,
Losing my leaves when it is fall.
But when it is spring, new leaves will show.
How do trees grow? Now you know!

33

Pollination

Hey, little hummingbird,
What are you haulin'?
Tiny little grains
That are known as pollen.
Hey, little honeybee,
What are you haulin'?
Tiny little grains
That are known as pollen.
Thanks, little hummingbird,
Thanks, honeybee.
By bringing the pollen,
Plants grow seeds!
Thanks, little honeybee,
Thanks, hummingbird.
You've brought the pollen,
Now what's the good word?
Pollination!

Fruits

In a giant fruit basket,
Here's what I found:
Grapes and grapefruit,
Plums, sweet and round.
Strawberries, blueberries,
Raspberries, too.
Dates and figs
As sticky as glue!
Apples and pineapples,
Cherries and pears.
Peaches with skin
With soft, fuzzy hairs.
Apricots, oranges,
A lemon and lime.
Watermelon, cantaloupe,
Fresh, in their prime.
Ripe bananas,
A juicy tangerine,
The tastiest fruit basket
I've ever seen!

Vegetables

Eat your vegetables,
Clean your plate!
Eat your vegetables,
Veggies are great!
String beans, broccoli,
Lettuce and peas,
Squash and brussels sprouts,
More corn, please!
Cucumbers, eggplant,
Beets and tomatoes,
Celery, carrots,
Spinach and potatoes.
Radishes, cauliflower,
Cabbage and cress,
Peppers and onions,
Asparagus? Yes!
Black beans, lima beans,
Soybeans, too.
Eat your veggies,
They're good for you!

Apple

(sung to "Bingo")

I know a fruit that grows on trees,
An apple is its name, oh!

CHORUS:
A-P-P-L-E,
A-P-P-L-E,
A-P-P-L-E,
An apple is its name, oh!

In summer and in early fall
It's time to pick an apple!

CHORUS

It may be sweet or may be tart,
It's red, or green, or yellow!

CHORUS

A McIntosh or Granny Smith,
A Winesap or Delicious!

CHORUS

Make applesauce or apple juice
Or apple pie with apples!

CHORUS

Pumpkin Patch

Look out, patch! Look out, ground!
Giant pumpkins are all around!
Starting from a tiny seed,
In just four months, they grow indeed!
The pumpkins get so round and fat,
Up to two hundred pounds—imagine that!
Clinging to a bush or vine,
So thick and orange, so sweet and fine!
The pumpkins grow in great supply,
I can't wait for pumpkin pie!

Food

Food makes you big,
Food makes you grow.
Food gives you energy
To go, go, go!

Food keeps you healthy,
Food keeps you well.
Food's good to taste
And good to smell!

Food makes you happy,
Food makes you strong.
Food's what you need
Your whole life long!

The World of Animals

Animals here, animals there,
Animal homes are everywhere!
High on a mountain slope so steep
Are the yak and panda, goat and sheep.
In the grasslands, flat and wide,
The zebra and giraffe abide.
In woodland forests near the water
You'll find the bear and moose and otter.
In tropical forests with lots of rain
The toucan and the sloth remain.
Out in the desert, hot and dry,
The camel and the snake go by.
In arctic regions filled with snow,
The polar bear and penguin go.
Deep in the ocean, a watery home,
The whale and shark and octopus roam,
Animals here, animals there,
Animal homes are everywhere!

Animal Talk

Ducks quack, bears growl,
Geese honk, wolves howl.
Hens cluck, horses neigh,
Bees buzz, donkeys bray.
Cats meow, dogs bark,
Birds chirp in the park.
Turkeys gobble, cows moo,
Tigers roar in the zoo.
Snakes hiss, pigs squeal,
Hyenas laugh a great deal.
Owls hoot, mice squeak,
Animals love to speak!

Underground Creatures

Who can be found
Underground?
Worms squirm
In the dirt.
Ants dig tunnels
Without getting hurt!
Groundhogs and moles
Make cozy holes.
Who can be found
Underground?
Lots of busy creatures!

Animal Homes

(sung to "On Top of Old Smoky")

On top of a mountain,
Or under the sea,
There are so many places
Where creatures may be.

Alone in a desert,
Or grouped on a farm,
Or tucked in a tree trunk
Away from all harm.

On bright, sunny grasslands,
Or in a dark cave,
In jungles and forests,
Where all must be brave.

On ice in the Arctic,
Or holed underground,
There are so many places
Where creatures are found!

Hibernation

(sung to "Alouette")

CHORUS:
Hibernation, time for hibernation,
Hibernation, time to go to sleep.

In the winter, where's the bear?
Sleeping in its log or lair.
Where's the bear? Log or lair. Oh!

CHORUS

In the winter, where's the frog?
Sleeping by a pond or log.
Where's the frog? Pond or log.
Where's the bear? Log or lair. Oh!

CHORUS

In the winter, where's the snake?
In the mud beneath the lake.
Where's the snake? In the lake.
Where's the frog? Pond or log.
Where's the bear? Log or lair. Oh!

CHORUS

In the winter, where's the bat?
In a cave is where it's at.
Where's the bat? A cave it's at.
Where's the snake? In the lake.
Where's the frog? Pond or log.
Where's the bear? Log or lair. Oh!

CHORUS

Baby Animals

(sung to "Mary Had a Little Lamb")

Sheep give birth to little lambs,
Little lambs, little lambs.
Sheep give birth to little lambs,
Yes, that's the baby's name.

Dogs and seals have little pups,
Little pups, little pups.
Dogs and seals have little pups,
Yes, that's the baby's name.

Cows and whales have little calves,
Little calves, little calves.
Cows and whales have little calves,
Yes, that's the baby's name.

Ostriches and hens have chicks,
Little chicks, little chicks.
Ostriches and hens have chicks,
Yes, that's the baby's name.

Bears and lions both have cubs,
Little cubs, little cubs.
Bears and lions both have cubs,
Yes, that's the baby's name.

Deer give birth to little fawns,
Little fawns, little fawns.
Deer give birth to little fawns,
Yes, that's the baby's name.

Antelope have little kids,
Little kids, little kids.
Antelope have little kids,
And people have kids, too!

Eggs

Eggs! Eggs!
Who lays eggs?
Hens lay eggs.
That I knew!
Only hens?
All birds do!
Only birds?
Not true!
Fish lay eggs
And quite a few!
Birds and fish
And insects, too!
And reptiles and
Amphibians do!
Who's in an egg?
Someone new!
Time to hatch!
Open, you
Eggs! Eggs! Eggs!

Animal Movement

(sung to "Goodnight, Ladies")

Hello, eagle, hello, robin,
Hello, sparrow, we love to watch you go!
Merrily you fly along, fly along, fly along,
Merrily you fly along,
Yes, that is how you move!

Hello, dolphin, hello, marlin,
Hello, salmon, we love to watch you go!
Merrily you swim along, swim along, swim along,
Merrily you swim along,
Yes, that is how you move!

Hello, beetle, hello, turtle,
Hello, inchworm, we love to watch you go!
Merrily you crawl along, crawl along, crawl along,
Merrily you crawl along,
Yes, that is how you move!

Hello, cricket, hello, rabbit,
Hello, froggy, we love to see you go!
Merrily you hop along, hop along, hop along,
Merrily you hop along,
Yes, that is how you move!

Hello, ostrich, hello, cheetah,
Hello, greyhound, we love to see you go!
Merrily you run along, run along, run along,
Merrily you run along,
Yes, that is how you move!

Animal Tracks

Animals, forward!
Now look back.
Can you identify
Each animal track?
Who has a hoof print?
Who has a paw?
Who has webbed feet?
Who has a claw?
Who has two legs?
Who has four?
Who has six legs?
Who has more?
Animals, forward!
Now step back.
Can you identify
Each animal track?

Animal Defenses

(sung to "Sing a Song of Sixpence")

Sing a song of defense,
Sharks use their jaws.
Porcupines have quills,
And bears kick with claws.
Moose rely on horns,
And snakes like to bite.
Clams shut up inside their shell
So they don't have to fight!

Rabbits hop away,
And birds fly off fast.
Octopuses shoot black ink
In a blast!
Eels give a shock,
And skunks make a stink.
Animals defend themselves
In more ways than you think!

Zoo

(sung to "Skip to My Lou")

CHORUS:
Zoo, zoo, who's in the zoo?
Zoo, zoo, who's in the zoo?
Zoo, zoo, who's in the zoo?
Who's in the zoo to visit?

Monkeys swinging on a tree,
Sheep and lions grazing free,
Tall giraffes, a sight to see!
All in the zoo to visit.

CHORUS

Deer with antlers on their head,
Hippos waiting to be fed,
Peacocks with their feathers spread,
All in the zoo to visit.

CHORUS

Polar bears all getting wet,
Baby goats that I can pet,
Elephants I won't forget,
All in the zoo to visit.

CHORUS

48

Animal Groups

Some animals
Live in a group.
A special name
Describes each troop:
A herd of cattle,
A gaggle of geese,
A flock of sheep
With woolly fleece.
A pride of lions,
A bevy of quails,
A litter of puppies
With wagging tails.
A school of fish,
A swarm of flies,
A pride of wolves
With watchful eyes.
A brood of hens,
A nest of birds,
Animal groups
With special words!

Mammals

Do you know mammals? Sure you do!
Dog and cat, to name just two.
Monkey, cow, zebra, camel,
Flying bat? Also a mammal!
Lion, tiger, mouse, and rat,
Whale and dolphin—did you know that?
Sheep and rabbit, goat and rhino,
(Do you know all the mammals I know?)
Giraffe, hippo, kangaroo,
Squirrel, bear, and even you!
Deer, porcupine, elephant, horse,
Do you know mammals? Of course, of course!

Amphibians

Living in water
Or living on land,
Being an amphibian
Must be grand!
If I were a frog,
Salamander, or toad,
I would jump in a lake
Or crawl on a road.
Living in water
Or living on land,
Being an amphibian
Must be grand!

Reptiles

Reptile, reptile,
Tell me why
Your skin is scaly
And so dry?
Alligator, crocodile,
Lizard, turtle, snake,
All day long
In the sun you bake.
Reptile, reptile,
I make a motion:
Pamper yourself
With body lotion!

Bugs

(sung to "When the Saints Go Marching In")

Oh, when the bugs go marching in,
Oh, when the bugs go marching in,
Oh, how I'll see the ants and the beetles,
Oh, when the bugs go marching in.

Oh, when the bugs begin to crawl,
Oh, when the bugs begin to crawl,
Oh, how I'll see the roaches and termites,
Oh, when the bugs begin to crawl.

Oh, when the bugs come flying in,
Oh, when the bugs come flying in,
Oh, how I'll see the moths and mosquitoes,
Oh, when the bugs come flying in.

Oh, when the bugs begin to buzz,
Oh, when the bugs begin to buzz,
Oh, how I'll hear the bees and cicadas,
Oh, when the bugs begin to buzz.

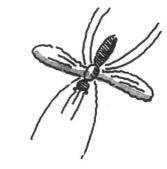

Oh, when the bugs begin to leap,
Oh, when the bugs begin to leap,
Oh, how I'll see the fleas and the crickets,
Oh, when the bugs begin to leap!

Birds

(sung to "Rock-a-Bye Baby in the Treetop")

Look at the bird
Up in the treetop,
Building its nest
With no time to stop.
Hatching its eggs
So smooth and so round,
Then feeding its babies
Worms from the ground.

Look at the bird
With beak for a mouth.
When it gets cold,
The bird will fly south.
When it gets warm,
The bird will return.
Let's watch how the birds live,
And see what we learn!

Penguin

I know a bird
That cannot fly:
Penguin is its name.
It cannot fly,
But it can swim
With speed that wins it fame!

I know a bird
That lives on ice
And waddles by the sea.
It looks so cute
In its black-and-white suit,
As handsome as can be!

Fish

How I wish
I were a fish!
My day would begin
Flapping my fins.
I'd make a commotion
Out in the ocean.
It would be cool
To swim in a school.
In the sea,
I'd move so free,
With just one thought:
Don't get caught!

Sea Creatures

Come along, come with me,
Take a dive in the deep blue sea.
Put on your gear, let's explore
All the way to the ocean floor!

See that snail wrapped in curls?
Look! An oyster wearing pearls!
Watch the octopus oh so dark,
But don't you dare to pet the shark!

Dive on down, seaward bound,
Motion in the ocean is all around!
Dive on down, seaward bound,
Motion in the ocean is all around!

Now we're very far below,
The lantern fish are all aglow.
Is that a tiny shock you feel?
You just met an electric eel!

Giant blue whales start to stir,
Bigger than dinosaurs ever were!
Wave good-bye to the squid and sponge,
This is the end of our deep-sea plunge!

Dive on down, seaward bound,
Motion in the ocean is all around!
Dive on down, seaward bound,
Motion in the ocean is all around!

Bear

Big bear, big bear,
Hunting near the trees.
Feasting on the honeycomb
Made by busy bees.

Big bear, big bear,
Wading in the lake.
Fish is your favorite dish:
Which one will you take?

Big bear, big bear,
Resting in your den.
Sleeping through the winter
Before coming out again!

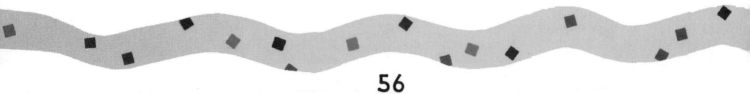

Cat Family

The cat family has many creatures,
And each one has special features.
The lion roams the jungle wide,
Wearing its shaggy mane with pride.
The tiger's coat has stripes so thin
To blend with grass it's hiding in!
The leopard wears a coat of spots,
As gracefully it leaps and trots.
The cheetah has a running gift.
No other cat is quite as swift.
The panther has a screeching cry,
Climbing mountains oh so high.
The jaguar has a forest home,
And in the night it likes to roam.
In your home, do cats roam free?
They're also part of the cat family!

Birth of a Butterfly

(sung to "Hush Little Baby, Don't Say a Word")

A mama butterfly lays all her eggs,
Out pops a caterpillar, crawling on its legs.

The caterpillar first is rather thin,
But then it eats till it bursts through its skin.

After growing nice and big,
The caterpillar climbs on a leaf or twig.

It makes a shell where it hangs inside.
The shell then cracks, and the parts divide.

Inside the shell, a change was going on,
The form of the caterpillar now is gone.

When the shell opens, what comes out?
A beautiful butterfly fluttering about!

Firefly

Firefly, firefly,
Wow, how you glow!
Under your body
You light up below!
Firefly, firefly,
Wow, how you shine!
At night in the dark
I can see you just fine!

Save Our Animals

Saving our animals
Really is important.
Every kind of animal
Needs a safe home.

When you see an animal,
Always treat it kindly.
Make its neighborhood
A safe place to roam!

Dinosaurs

(sung to "Pussycat, Pussycat")

Dinosaurs, dinosaurs,
Where have you been?
I've only seen you
In books that you're in.
Dinosaurs, dinosaurs,
Why aren't you here?
I want to know what
Made you all disappear!

Dinosaurs, dinosaurs,
How you would roam!
Forests and beaches
Were your private home.
Dinosaurs, dinosaurs,
How you could eat!
Dining on plant life
Or dining on meat.

Dinosaurs, dinosaurs,
Where did you go?
Once you were giants,
And how you did grow!
Dinosaurs, dinosaurs,
What made you die?
So many guesses,
But no one's sure why.

My Body

(sung to "My Bonnie Lies Over the Ocean")

My body makes all kinds of motion,
My body makes motion you see.
My body makes all kinds of motion,
My body makes motion for me!

CHORUS:
Jump, twirl, bend, whirl,
My body is moving for me, for me.
Jump, twirl, bend, whirl,
My body is moving for me.

My body can run up a mountain,
My body can skip down the street.
My body can make many motions,
I think that my body is neat!

CHORUS

61

Five Senses

(sung to "If You're Happy and You Know It")

When you look and when you see, use your eyes.
When you look and when you see, use your eyes.
When you look and when you see
All the things there are to see,
When you look and when you see, use your eyes!

When you listen and you hear, use your ears.
When you listen and you hear, use your ears.
When you listen and you hear
All the things there are to hear,
When you listen and you hear, use your ears!

When you touch and when you feel, use your hands.
When you touch and when you feel, use your hands.
When you touch and when you feel
All the things there are to feel,
When you touch and when you feel, use your hands!

When you eat and when you taste, use your tongue.
When you eat and when you taste, use your tongue.
When you eat and when you taste
All the things there are to taste,
When you eat and when you taste, use your tongue!

When you sniff and when you smell, use your nose.
When you sniff and when you smell, use your nose.
When you sniff and when you smell
All the things there are to smell,
When you sniff and when you smell, use your nose!

Fingers and Hands

(sung to "Ten Little Indians")

CHORUS:
One little, two little, three little fingers,
Four little, five little, six little fingers,
Seven little, eight little, nine little fingers,
Ten little fingers on two hands!

On each hand I've got a thumb
Plus four more fingers that become
Five fingers, so the total sum
Is ten little fingers on two hands!

CHORUS

My two hands and fingers ten
Can hold a spoon or hold a pen,
Or lend a helping hand, my friend!
I've ten little fingers on two hands!

CHORUS

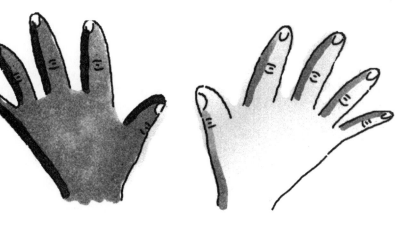

Brain

Use your brain
To help explain
All the thoughts
In your head.
Use your mind
To help you find
The words that need
To be said!

Skin

What covers my arms, legs, and chin?
Skin!
What protects each ankle and shin?
Skin!
What's layered so it isn't too thin?
Skin!
What helps keep my body parts in?
Skin?
What stretches whenever I grin?
Skin!

Bones

(sung to "Home on the Range")

Oh, give me some bones
That are sturdy as stones,
That connect from my head to my toes.
My bones help me out,
Help my body about,
They protect it wherever it goes!

CHORUS:
Bones, bones hard and strong,
All connected so nothing goes wrong.
My bones help me out,
Help my body about,
Bones protect me as I go along!

The bones in my spine
Help me stand up just fine,
While the bones in my ribs guard my heart.
The bones in my hips
Let me sit or do dips.
Without bones, I would just fall apart!

CHORUS

Heart and Blood

(sung to "The Ants Go Marching One By One")

The heart is pumping blood for us,
Hurrah, hurrah!
The heart's a muscle fabulous,
Hurrah, hurrah!
The heart is pumping blood for us,
It pumps all day without a fuss,
And the blood goes round
Because of our pumping heart!

The blood supplies us oxygen,
Hurrah, hurrah!
It's what our body needs to run,
Hurrah, hurrah!
The blood supplies us oxygen,
And that's a need for everyone,
And the blood goes round
Because of our pumping heart!

Breathing

Breathe in!
Breathe out!
Breathe in!
Breathe out!

All day
Air goes
In your lungs,
Out your nose.

Inhale!
Exhale!
Inhale!
Exhale!

Wide awake,
Fast asleep,
Day and night,
You keep

Breathing in,
Breathing out.
You don't even
Think about

Breathing in,
Breathing free.
Breathe
Involuntarily!

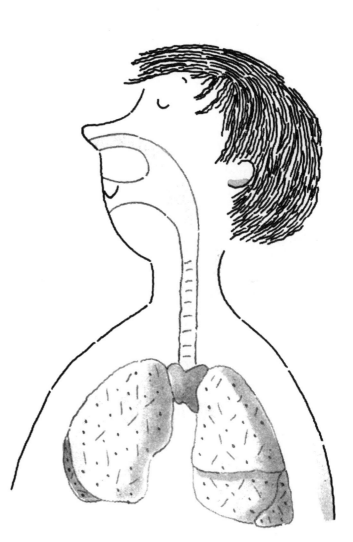

Digestion

Chomp, chomp! Chew, chew!
When you eat, what do you do?
Chomp, chomp! Chew, chew!
Till it's time to swallow.

Gulp, gulp! Swallow, swallow!
Down into the stomach hollow.
Gulp, gulp! Swallow, swallow!
There the food is stored.

Mix, mix! Churn, churn!
Juices mix as muscles turn.
Mix, mix! Churn, churn!
The food is breaking down.

Sugar, starch, protein, fat,
Your body uses all of that.
Sugar, starch, protein, fat
That your food provides!

That's the process.
One last question:
What's this process called?
Digestion!

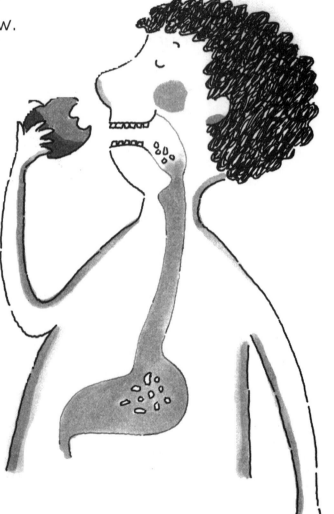

Growing

If you'd like to know
What makes you grow,
The answer I'll tell:
A single cell!
As the cell multiplies,
You grow bigger in size!

Germs

Wash your face and hands with soap,
Wash them every day.
Keeping clean by using soap
Will help keep germs away!

Stay Healthy

How do you stay healthy?
Eat right! Sleep right!
Exercise to keep right!

Just as cars need gas to go,
You need food to run and grow!
So many foods to eat, it's true!
Which ones are the best for you?

Food alone is not enough.
Exercise also keeps you tough.
So many ways to work out, it's true.
What kind of exercise do you do?

Food and exercise aren't enough.
Rest also keeps you healthy and tough.
How many hours do you sleep at night?
Get enough rest, so you'll feel right!

How do you stay healthy?
Eat right! Sleep right!
Exercise to keep right!

Seasons of the Year

(sung to "Here We Go Round the Mulberry Bush")

CHORUS:
Here we go round the year again,
The year again, the year again.
Here we go round the year again,
To greet the different seasons.

Wintertime is time for snow.
To the south, the birds will go.
It's too cold for plants to grow
Because it is the winter.

CHORUS

In the springtime, days grow warm.
On the plants, the new buds form.
Bees and bugs come out to swarm
Because it is the spring.

CHORUS

In summertime, the days are hot.
Ice cold drinks I drink a lot!
At the beach, I've got a spot
Because it is the summer.

CHORUS

Fall is here, the air is cool.
Days are short, it's back to school.
Raking leaves is now the rule
Because it is the autumn.

CHORUS

Winter

Brrr! It's winter!
Makes me shake!
Snow on the ground
And ice on the lake!
Look what's falling!
Another snowflake!
A big round snowman
Is what I'll make!
Some nice hot cocoa
Is what I'll take!
Don't even think about
Ice cream cake!
Brrr! It's winter!
Give me a break!

Spring

What springs
In spring?
Buds spring!
Leaves spring!
Flowers spring!
Trees spring!
Plants spring!
Grass springs!
Robins sing
In spring!

Summer

Do you like summer?
I sure do!
Come to the beach,
I'll swim with you.
Let's hunt for seashells
Along the shore.
The beach in summer
Is great to explore!
Bring a pail and shovel
And give me a hand,
We'll build a castle
In the sand.
Do you like summer?
I sure do!
Come to the beach,
I'll play with you!

Fall

From September
To December,
What's the season?
Fall!
Red leaves start to
Fall!
Brown leaves start to
Fall!
Gold leaves start to
Fall!
Orange leaves start to
Fall!
Yellow leaves start to
Fall.
After all, it's
Fall!

Weather

Weather is hot,
Weather is cold,
Weather is changing
As the weeks unfold.

Skies are cloudy,
Skies are fair,
Skies are changing
In the air.

It is raining,
It is snowing,
It is windy
With breezes blowing.

Days are foggy,
Days are clear,
Weather is changing
Throughout the year!

Wind

Whoosh! Whoosh!
Whoosh!
Feel the wind push!
Blow! Blow! Blow!
Where'd my hat go?

Cloud

What is fluffy?
What is white?
What can you see
When skies are bright?
What can float?
What brings rain?
What may be higher
Than a bird or plane?
Say it out loud:
Cloud!

Thunder and Lightning

(sung to "Pop Goes the Weasel")

When a storm begins in the clouds,
It sometimes may look frightening.
You see a quick electrical spark—
Flash! goes the lightning!

Long and thin and streaky and fast,
Its glow is oh so brightening.
Watch for the electric spark—
Flash! goes the lightning!

When a storm begins in the clouds,
It truly is a wonder.
You hear a rumble loud in the sky—
Clap! goes the thunder!

Lightning bolts are heating the air,
Over clouds and under.
When the air expands enough—
Clap! goes the thunder.

Rain

(sung to "It Ain't Gonna' Rain No More, No More")

It is gonna' rain some more, some more,
It is gonna' rain some more!
When drops of water start to pour,
It is gonna' rain some more, some more!

Why do drops of water pour?
Drops of water pour?
The clouds can't hold them anymore,
That's why drops of water pour!

It is gonna' rain some more, some more,
It is gonna' rain some more!
When drops of water start to pour,
It is gonna' rain some more, some more!

Rainbow

(sung to "There's a Hole in the Bucket")

There's an arc in a rainbow,
So pretty, so pretty.
There's an arc in a rainbow,
With colors you see.

The sun after rain
Makes the colors, the colors.
The sun after rain
Makes the colors you see.

There's red and there's orange
And there's yellow so pretty.
There's red and there's orange
And there's yellow you see.

There's green and there's blue
And there's violet so pretty.
There's green and there's blue
And there's violet you see.

There's an arc in a rainbow,
So pretty, so pretty.
There's an arc in a rainbow,
With colors you see!

Water Cycle

(sung to "It's Raining, It's Pouring")

It's raining, it's pouring,
The oceans are storing
Water from the falling rain
While thunderclouds are roaring.

The rain now is stopping,
The rain's no longer dropping.
Sun comes out and soaks up water
Like a mop that's mopping.

The water's still there now,
But hidden in the air now.
In the clouds it makes a home
Until there's rain to share now.

It's raining, it's pouring...

Snow

Tiny ice crystals
In freezing weather,
Tiny ice crystals
Sticking together.
What do they make?
A single snowflake!

Ice

(sung to "Three Blind Mice")

We find ice, we find ice,
Where it is cold, where it is cold.
When the temperature drops to 32 degrees,
That's when water starts to freeze,
And frozen water guarantees
That we find ice!

We find ice, we find ice,
Inside the fridge, inside the fridge.
Ice is there, but did you know
That frost and sleet and hail and snow
Are also forms of ice, it's so!
Oh, we find ice!

Icicles

I see icy icicles
Hanging off the trees.
I see icy icicles
Forming in the freeze!
Here, oh here's the way
That an icicle will form:
A stream of water drips
While the air is still warm.
When the air turns colder
And water starts to freeze,
It forms a stick of ice
That hangs from the trees!
I see icy icicles!

Electricity

What power
Helps you and me?
The answer's
Electricity!

What makes light
So we can see?
The answer's
Electricity!

What gives machines
Their energy?
The answer's
Electricity!

What makes heat
So we live comfortably?
The answer's
Electricity!

Magnet

(sung to "Did You Ever See a Lassie?")

CHORUS:
Did you ever see a magnet,
A magnet, a magnet?
Did you ever see a magnet
Pull this way and that?

On iron and steel,
Its pull is unreal!
Did you ever see a magnet
Pull this way and that?

CHORUS

A magnet has action,
It's called an attraction!
Did you ever see a magnet
Pull this way and that?

CHORUS

Sound

Pssst!

Have you heard what's going around?
Sound!

Do you know how sound behaves?
It travels in invisible waves.

How do you know the waves are there?
They vibrate through the air.

When the waves reach our ear,
Sound is what we hear!

Pssst!

Have you heard what's going around?
Sound!

Echo

In a valley, valley, valley,
Or a canyon, canyon, canyon,
Give a shout, shout, shout
To find out, out, out
If there's an echo, echo, echo
In the air, air, air.
Sound will bounce, bounce, bounce
Off surfaces there, there, there.
You'll hear an echo, echo, echo,
Echo, echo, echo, echo...

Light

(sung to "Lullaby and Good Night")

See the light,
Very bright.
Do you know where light comes from?
Number one:
From the sun,
Yes, the sun in the sky gives light.
Number two:
Candles do,
So do light bulbs and flashlights.
And, of course,
As a source,
All the stars in the sky give light.

See the light,
Very bright,
Do you know how light helps us?
We can see,
You'll agree,
All because of a thing called light.
Light, you know,
Helps plants grow,
And we need plants for living.
Light gives heat,
Can't be beat.
Yes, we definitely need light!

Shadow

(sung to "Oh Dear, What Can the Matter Be?")

CHORUS:
Oh dear, where can my shadow be?
All day long, how it followed me!
But now, darkness is all I see,
And now my shadow is gone.

My shadow appeared as I was waking,
The sun shone on me as daylight was breaking,
The sun shone on me, and soon it was making
A beautiful shadow of me!

CHORUS

All day in the sun, all day I kept going,
My shadow was there, my shadow was growing,
But later, the night was no longer showing
That beautiful shadow of me!

Reflection

In a mirror,
What do I see?
Me!

In a pool of water,
What do I see?
Me!

In a silver spoon,
What do I see?
Me?

Is it really me?
A closer inspection
Shows me that it's
Just my reflection!!

Machine Song

Wheels are turning,
Blades are churning,
Rods are stirring,
Motors are purring,
Springs are coiling,
Oil is oiling,
Pins are pinging,
Machines are singing!

Flight

Why do birds have wings?
Tell me why, why, why!
Why do birds have wings?
So they can fly, fly, fly!
Where do they go with wings?
To the sky, sky, sky!
Airplanes too have wings
To go high, high, high!
If only I had wings,
Me oh my, my, my!

Gravity

(sung to "London Bridge Is Falling Down")

CHORUS:
Gravity is pulling down,
Pulling down, pulling down,
Gravity is pulling down
All around you!

Take a ball and toss it high.
Will it stay in the sky?
Gravity will pull it down
All around you.

CHORUS

Jump up high and down you'll go.
There's a force down below.
Gravity is pulling down
All around you.

CHORUS

Water

Water, water everywhere, water all around,
Water in the ocean, water in the ground.

Water in a river, water in a creek,
Water in a faucet with a drip-drip leak!

Water in a fountain, water in a lake,
Water on a flower, as day begins to break.

Water from a waterfall, rushing down from high,
Water from a dark cloud, raining from the sky.

Water boiling hot, water frozen ice,
Water in a blue lagoon, clean and clear and nice.

Water at a fire, gushing through a hose,
Water in a garden, so every flower grows.

Water for the animals swimming in the sea,
Water, water everywhere for you and for me!

Floating and Sinking

Why do things float?
Why do things sink?
What do you think?
What do you think?
Things that float
Are lighter than water.
That's why they float.
That's why they float.
Things that sink
Are heavier than water.
That's why they sink.
That's why they sink.

Bubbles

(sung to "Miss Lucy Had a Baby")

If you see any bubbles,
Do you know why they're there?
If you see any bubbles,
They're there because of air!

The outside of a bubble
Is very, very thin.
It stretches even thinner,
Whenever air gets in.

You often see a bubble
Inside a soapy sink.
But then before you know it,
It's gone in just a wink!

The bubble's skin is stretching
Until it has to stop.
When it can stretch no further,
The bubble goes POP!

POP

Recycling

(sung to "There Were Ten in the Bed")

A can in the bin
And another went in.
Recycle! Recycle!
We all recycled and added a can,
There were two in the bin and another went in.
Recycle! Recycle!
We all recycled and added a can,
There were three in the bin and another went in.
Recycle! Recycle!
We all recycled and added a can,
There were four in the bin and another went in.
Recycle! Recycle!
We all recycled and added a can,
There were five in the bin and another went in.
Recycle!!

Book Links

The Earth and Beyond

FICTION

The Great Kapok Tree by Lynne Cherry, 1990, Harcourt Brace.

The Moon Was at a Fiesta by Matthew Gollub, 1994, Tambourine.

How the Sea Began by George Crespo, 1993, Clarion.

NONFICTION

Rain Forest by Barbara Taylor, 1992, Dorling Kindersley.

The Moon Seems to Change by Franklyn M. Branley, 1989, HarperCollins.

Our Solar System by Seymour Simon, 1988, Morrow.

Rocks and Minerals by Steve Parker, 1993, Dorling Kindersley.

Plants and Seeds

FICTION

A Plant Called Spot by Nancy J. Peteraf, 1994, Doubleday.

Something Is Growing by Walter L. Krudop, 1995, Simon and Schuster.

Someday a Tree by Eve Bunting, 1993, Clarion.

Grandma's Garden by Elaine Moore, 1990, Lee & Shepard.

NONFICTION

From Seed to Plant by Gail Gibbons, 1991, Holiday House.

Pollinating a Flower by Paul Bennett, 1994, Thomson Learning.

The Reason for a Flower by Ruth Heller, 1883, Grosset & Dunlap.

Animals, Animals

FICTION

Bird Dogs Can't Fly by Mary Jane Auch, 1993, Holiday House.

If Anything Ever Goes Wrong at the Zoo by Mary Jean Hendrick, 1993, Harcourt Brace.

One Small Fish by Joanne Ryder, 1993, Morrow.

NONFICTION

Horns, Antlers, Fangs, and Tusks and Skin, Scales, Feathers, and Fur by Mark J. Rauzon, 1993, Lee & Shepard.

A Time for Babies by Ron Hirschi, 1993, Cobblehill.

Outstanding Outsides by Hana Machotka, 1993, Morrow.

The Human Body

FICTION

Avocado Baby by John Burningham, 1982, HarperCollins.

NONFICTION

Germs Make Me Sick! by Melvin Berger, 1985, HarperCollins.

Looking at the Body by David Suzuki, 1991, John Wiley & Sons.

What Happens to a Hamburger? by Paul Showers, 1989, Crowell.

Your Insides by Joanna Cole, 1992, Putnam Grosset.

My Five Senses by Aliki, 1989, HarperCollins.

Seasons and Weather

FICTION

First Snow, Magic Snow by John Cech, 1992, Four Winds.

The Same Wind by Bette Killion, 1992, HarperCollins.

Sam Panda and Thunder Dragon by Chris Conover, 1992, Farrar, Straus and Giroux.

Windsongs and Rainbows by Albert Burton, 1993, Simon and Schuster.

NONFICTION

Weather Forecasting by Gail Gibbons, 1987, Aladdin.

Sky Words by Marilyn Singer, 1994, Macmillan.

Rain & Hail by Franklyn M. Branley, 1983, HarperCollins.

More Science Wonders

FICTION

The Great Trash Bash by Leedy Loreen, 1991, Holiday House.

No Problem by Eileen Browne, 1993, Candlewick Press.

NONFICTION

Cartons, Cans and Orange Peels: Where Does Your Garbage Go? by Joanna Foster, 1991, Clarion.

Recycle! A Handbook for Kids by Gail Gibbons, 1992, Little, Brown and Company.

Simple Machines by Ann Horvatic, 1989, E.P. Dutton.

The Science Book of Sound by Neil Ardley, 1991, Harcourt Brace Jovanovich.

Switch On, Switch Off by Melvin Berger, 1989, Thomas Y. Crowell.

Gravity Is a Mystery by Franklyn M. Branley, 1986, HarperCollins.